piano • vocal • guitar

house of love

S0-DYU-944

ISBN 0-7935-3904-8

HAL•LEONARD
CORPORATION
7777 W. BLUEMOUND RD. P.O. BOX 13819 MILWAUKEE, WI 53213

LUCKY ONE

Words and Music by AMY GRANT
and KEITH THOMAS

You're the kind ___ when you
You're the kind ___ that I

ba - by, I'm the luck - y one. _____

SAY YOU'LL BE MINE

Words and Music by AMY GRANT,
WAYNE KIRKPATRICK and KEITH THOMAS

WHATEVER IT TAKES

Words and Music by AMY GRANT,
GARY CHAPMAN and KEITH THOMAS

Moderate ballad tempo

20

HOUSE OF LOVE

Words and Music by WALLY WILSON,
KENNY GREENBERG and GREG BARNHILL

THE POWER

Words and Music by JUDSON SPENCE
and TOMMY SIMS

34

OH, HOW THE YEARS GO BY

Words and Music by SIMON CLIMIE
and WILL JENNINGS

BIG YELLOW TAXI

Words and Music by
JONI MITCHELL

HELPING HAND

Words and Music by AMY GRANT,
TOMMY SIMS and BEVERLY DARNALL

LOVE HAS A HOLD ON ME

Words and Music by AMY GRANT
and KEITH THOMAS

I have found the per - fect
As I'm look-ing down the

mys - ter - y,   love has   a   hold   on me.
road a - head,   love has   a   hold   on me.

OUR LOVE

Words and Music by AMY GRANT
and TOM HEMBY

*Vocal written one octave higher than sung.

CHILDREN OF THE WORLD

Words and Music by AMY GRANT,
WAYNE KIRKPATRICK and TOMMY SIMS

*Vocal written one octave higher than sung.